The Grey Tale of Mrs Sciurus

The Grey Tale of Mrs Sciurus

by Dr Colin Bonnington

First published in 2018 by Dr Colin Bonnington

Illustrations copyright © Colin Bonnington
Front and back covers designed by Chris Freeman

ISBN 978-1-9999394-0-3

A catalogue record of this book is available from the British Library.

Any resemblance to persons fictional or real, living or dead, is purely coincidental.

This story is for all of my family.

I want to dedicate the tale to my grandad, who, although recently gone, will be forever in my thoughts.

Chapter 1
Eviction

The autumnal sun rose in the east, spilling wondrous light over the sprawling countryside. The landscape was a mosaic of arable fields, some wheat, some barley and some oats, criss-crossed by dense, lush hedges. Chestnut, beech and oak trees, scattered out along the hedge-lines, were adorned with their brittle amber-shaded leaves which rustled in the gentle breeze. A mixed flock of finches flew between trees, two rabbits sat quietly nibbling on frost-edged grassy tussocks and a distant sheep bleated.

Suddenly, another sound cut through the orchestral sounds of the countryside - a much more rapid and decisive sound of stomping. The finches swiftly flew off and the rabbits disappeared down their burrows. At the end of the field, two figures, darkened by the shadow of a hedge next to them, moved purposely along the edge. As they passed a gate, the sunlight revealed that these were two hares. One of them, with a damaged, scruffy ear, carried a wooden board. When they came to a large oak tree they stopped and looked up. There, near the summit of the tree, perhaps around fifteen metres into the air, and wedged between forked branches, was a ball of twigs and dead, brown leaves; the Sciurus family home, or rather, the drey.

'Yeah this is the one,' the scruffy-eared hare said, standing by the base. He produced a mallet and, holding the wooden board in place, he hammered a nail into the oak's trunk and secured the board with a piece of string. 'Right, that's us done here…for now anyway,' he said, looking rather pleased with himself. He stepped back and admired the sign. Then, the hares turned swiftly and moved away.

The sign hung menacingly from the trunk and read:

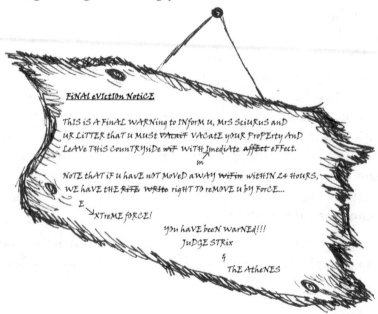

FiNAL eVIctIOn NotiCE

ThIS iS A FinAL WARNing to INforM u, MrS SciuRuS anD UR LiTTER thaT u MuSt ~~VAcaiF~~ VAcatE youR ProPErty AnD LeAVe ThiS CounTRYsiDe ~~wiF~~ WiTH ImediAte ~~affEct~~ eFFect.

NoTE thAT iF u hAVE nOT MoVeD aWAY ~~wiFin~~ witHIN 24 HouRS, WE hAVE tHE ~~RiTE~~ ~~WRIte~~ rigHT TO reMOVE u by ForCE…

XTreME fORCE!

You hAVE beeN WarNEd!!!
JuDGE STRix
&
ThE AtheNES

8

Chapter 2
Batten Down the Hatches

Mrs Sciurus poked her head out of the drey and was instantly covered in early morning sunlight. 'What a beautiful morning,' she thought, stretching. She moved back into her home where her three babies, Pip, Kip and Nip, were stirring from their sleeps.

'Morning, little ones.'

'Morning mum,' the babies replied together, rubbing their eyes.

'Did you all sleep well?'

'Yeah, Mum, but is it not too early to get up?' Kip whined as he turned back over.

'My love. This is the best part of the day and it's beautiful outside. We should all be out enjoying it, bright-eyed and bushy-tailed. I'll pop out and bring back some breakfast. How do crab-apples sound?'

'Yeah!' Pip cried out, and he started to leap up and down with excitement.

With that, Mrs Sciurus climbed out of the drey and down the side of the grand oak. When she reached the ground she noticed the sign. She read it glumly and tears started to well in her eyes. She wiped them away.

'Oh no, we've nowhere else to go,' she sighed.

She turned around and made for the bottom hedge, where a crooked crab-apple tree stood. Wind-fallen apples littered the ground beneath. She gathered all she could and scurried back to her home. She quickly clambered up the oak tree and into the drey.

'Right little ones...' she said, as she dropped the fruit onto the floor. 'Change of plan. We'll be staying inside now for the rest of the day.'

'But, Mum, I thought you said it was beautiful outside?'

'It's actually a bit colder than I first thought,' she fibbed, trying to control her nerves. 'In fact, I think we should block this window to stop the chill coming in...' She shifted uneasily. 'Or anything else unwanted for that matter.'

Chapter 3
Knock, Knock...Who's There?

Mrs Sciurus wasn't sure what time it was. There was no light coming into the drey, now that she had blocked up the window with a bit of a branch she had collected from beneath the grand oak.

The four squirrels had been sitting in the dark for maybe a day, Mrs Sciurus guessed. And the game of 'I Spy' hadn't lasted that long after 'Something beginning with D' had been used. Instead, she told her children stories about their father and how happy he would have been to see how they'd turned out, all three of them.

Pip, Kip and Nip were now sleeping soundly, if their snores were anything to go by, when Mrs Sciurus suddenly heard a voice, a stern voice, from outside.

'Oi, Grey-tail!' There was a short pause 'We are here to move you and your family from these premises, this area and this countryside. IMMEDIATELY!'

'Oh no,' Mrs Sciurus whispered, moving quickly to her children.

'We know you're in there. We have the right to come up and move you by force if necessary, but we'd rather you'd come peacefully.'

A few minutes passed and Mrs Sciurus stood stock still in the dark, hardly daring to breathe.

'Right, if you want to play it like that...' came the voice. 'We're coming up to get you!'

Mrs Sciurus almost jumped out of her grey fur and she gave out a huge breath. She frantically moved around the drey. 'Little ones, please, you must wake up,' she whispered, feeling her way in the dark and gently nudging them one after another.

'Awwww, Muuuuummmmmm,' moaned one of them, probably Kip.

Just then there was an almighty crash on the branch blocking the window, then rapid drumming.

'Oh my!'

'Mum, what's going on?' one of the babies cried out.

'It's OK, little ones, Mum's here. We'll be OK,' she replied, although her heart was racing. The children moved around their mum and cuddled her tightly, scared stiff, every one of them.

All of a sudden, the branch disintegrated and daylight shot into the drey. Mrs Sciurus put her hand over her face and pulled her little ones in tightly, as sawdust, splinters and other bits of debris filled her home.

'What do you think you're doing?' she called out.

'We really wish you'd come peacefully!' shrieked the large black and white woodpecker who now filled the entrance to the drey. Mrs Sciurus moved back from the intruder and clutched Pip, Kip and Nip.

'Right...' the large bird smirked moving forward. 'Who's coming first?'

Chapter 4
The House Goes Boom

First, the woodpecker pecked at Mrs Sciurus. She tried to dodge the bird's gigantic beak, but the woodpecker then flapped its wings wildly, causing confusion. While Mrs Sciurus was distracted, the bird managed to pinch her tail. He grabbed it and pulled it towards the entrance.

He was strong and she had a thought, as she was man-handled, or indeed squirrel-handled, that it didn't appear to be the first time that he had done this. Mrs Sciurus was now facing her children with the woodpecker outside the drey pulling her backwards by the tail.

'Don't worry, my loves!' she called. 'I'll see you at the bottom.' With that she was pulled clean out of her home. Pip, Kip and Nip looked at each other.

The woodpecker dropped Mrs Sciurus and she landed on the ground. Before she even had time to look around and assess her options, she was grabbed roughly by two hares.

'It would've been a lot easier if you had come quietly...' the scruffy-eared hare said with a sly smile. 'Mind you...' he added, 'it always makes it more interesting when you lot do play up.' One of the other hares gave a snort.

'Right, now get the young ones!' he cried, looking up at the drey. The woodpecker shot back into the squirrel's home and reappeared with all three little ones dangling by their tails from the great pied bird's big beak.

'Get off me, I'm tired!' Kip called.

'I'll bite you!' Nip added.

'I'm hungry!' Pip finished off.

Mrs Sciurus was reunited with her babies again, but this time they were surrounded by a hoard of horrible hares.

'Destroy the house!' the scruffy-eared hare ordered, as he pointed up to the drey.

'No!' Mrs Sciurus cried, but it was no good. The woodpecker landed next to their house and started to peck wildly on the side. Before long, the walls started to fall apart and the squirrel family and the hares on the ground below were showered in pieces of twigs and leaves. Within a few minutes, Mrs Sciurus's home was a home no more. She hugged her little ones and swallowed hard, trying to suppress her tears. This had been her and Mr Sciurus's marital home and she had strong memories of their time together here. These memories suddenly felt very blurred though, as she looked at the debris now scattered across the ground.

'Good, good!' the scruffy-eared hare called out. 'Now let's get them down to Judge Strix. I'm sure he'll be delighted to see them all,' he said with a smirk, as the party moved away from the large oak tree.

As they walked away, Mrs Sciurus peered back over her shoulder at the tree which had supported their home, and kept watching it, until it was no bigger than a pot plant, then no bigger than a stem of asparagus, then no bigger than a weed and then... and then, it was gone.

Chapter 5
Guilty Before Charged

The lead hare gripped Mrs Sciurus's shoulder roughly as he marched her passed hedge after hedge and through field after field.

'Do you have to be so rough?' she asked.

'Just be quiet and keep moving!' he shot back.

Pip, Kip and Nip held onto their mum tightly as the group moved through the countryside at a considerable pace.

'Can we go a little slower?' she asked. 'It's just that my little ones are struggling—'

'I said be quiet!' the lead hare interrupted. 'They can struggle all they want. I'm not interested!'

Meanwhile, in a marvellous hollowed-out chestnut tree, sat a large owl. He sat proudly on a wooden perch, which had the words *Judge Strix* carved into it. Beneath the large owl sat three little owls that perched on wooden protrusions carved with *The Athenes*.

Directly beneath the owls stood a trio of songbirds: a robin, a nuthatch and a great tit. The robin looked visibly nervous, shuffling from side to side. Finally, opposite the three birds, stood a group of animals, consisting of a hedgehog, an otter, a water vole and a red squirrel.

There was a noise from outside the tree.

'I think they're here,' Judge Strix announced. The

little owls sat up slightly and all eyes were directed to the entrance. The scruffy-eared hare pushed Mrs Sciurus harshly in the back and she stumbled into the hollow. The hare guards followed her in. The group came to a halt in the middle of the hollowed-out room.

The scruffy-eared hare cleared his throat and looked up to Judge Strix. 'I bring you Mrs Sciurus and her litter,' he announced, tipping his head slightly.

'Very good, Lieutenant Lepus, sterling job.' Judge Strix lifted a wing towards the entrance. 'You may step back.'

'Very well, judge,' Lepus replied, and he led the other hares to the hollow entrance, where they all took up their positions.

'Mrs Sciurus. Mrs Caroline Sciurus, if I'm not mistaken. Good morning,' Judge Strix called down.

'Is it?' she replied.

'There's no need to be like that!' the judge boomed. 'Not in my court!'

Mrs Sciurus shrugged in a dejected fashion.

'Anyway...' Suddenly Judge Strix started to cough compulsively. Everyone watched in anticipation. The little owls looked up eagerly at the larger owl. He raised a wing in reassurance and, after a few more coughs, produced a pellet (about the size of your little finger). 'Apologies,' he uttered, clearing his throat and placing the dark pellet on the ledge by his side. 'Where was I? Oh yes. You, Mrs Sciurus, have received a number of requests to leave your home, and indeed this countryside, all of which have been ignored.'

Mrs Sciurus looked at her young ones, clutched them tightly and peered back up at the judge. 'But this is our home, and it's all we know. Don't you think we have as much right to live here as everyone else?'

'Well, with all due respect, that's your opinion, Mrs Sciurus, and it is not a view that the vast majority of animals living in this countryside share. You see, you're an outsider, an intruder, and one who has overstayed her welcome, for about 150 years!' the judge barked.

'But I was born here, just like you, and you and you,' she said, turning and looking at the other animals in the room.

'Hold on there. You might've been, but your distant relatives weren't. They were American. North American! You're not truly English like me, or Mrs Vulgaris the squirrel down there, or Mr Lutra the otter, or The Athenes.'

'Excuse me?! The Athenes?! Their distant relatives weren't born here either, so how's that any different?' Mrs Sciurus exclaimed, looking at the little owls and back to Judge Strix. The little owls squirmed, almost falling off their perches.

'Ehm...' Judge Strix replied. 'It just is different. Us owls stick together, and anyway don't talk back!'

'Now...' he announced. He cleared his throat. 'I would like to welcome everyone... well ... almost everyone...' he said, glaring down at the family of grey squirrels, '...to this magnificent court, Judge Strix's court. I would like to invite Mrs Rubecula, Mr Sitta and Major Parus up to speak please.' He looked down at the robin, nuthatch and great tit and, with the wave of a wing, he beckoned them forward. 'All three have very intriguing stories about Mrs Sciurus which I'm sure you'll all be dying to hear!'

Chapter 6
All Wings Point to Mrs Sciurus

The three birds moved tentatively out from the shadows, none more so than the robin, Mrs Rubecula, who shifted uneasily. Judge Strix called down to her to compose herself and to begin her story when she was ready.

'I want ... to tell you about ...' stammered Mrs Rubecula. She stopped and swallowed harshly. 'About what these squirrels ... these vile grey squirrels ... have done to my family!' She stopped, keeping her eyes looking at the ground.

'It's OK, Mrs Rubecula, take your time,' Judge Strix reassured from above.

'This monster!' The robin pointed directly at Mrs Sciurus, but didn't look at her. She regained her composure and cried, 'Took all my eggs and ate them! She has left me with nothing!' Tears began to pour down her face.

'I didn't take your eggs, Mrs Rubecula, I promise! I would never have done that!' Mrs Sciurus called out. 'Please look at me!' she pleaded, stepping forward towards the robin.

'I don't want to look at you!' the robin cried. She looked in the opposite direction and raised her wings to cover her face.

Judge Strix cried out, 'Ehm, excuse me. Major Dendrocopos and Minor Dendrocopos, please.'

Instantly, the large pied woodpecker Mrs Sciurus recognised from earlier appeared, along with another, which was much smaller but with quite similar colourations - a black and white body and a red crown on its head - stepped between the robin and the grey squirrels to protect the red-breasted witness.

Next, Judge Strix, called up the other witnesses, Mr Sitta, the nuthatch and Major Parus, the great tit, to testify against Mrs Sciurus.

'I was quietly going about my business, scurrying up and down my favourite tree and pecking at insects for my breakfast, when I noticed that large parts of the bark had been ripped clean off. Mrs Sciurus was sure to have done it,' Mr Sitta declared.

Then Major Parus announced, 'As normal, myself and the other tit squadron, Captain Cyanistes and Pilot Periparus, visited our local feeding station last week, when suddenly we realised that there was no food left for us to refuel. No nuts, no seeds, no nothing. Not only that, but the feeder had been broken so it could no longer hold any food. Someone had chewed and damaged it so that the food had all fallen out and then they had guzzled it all up and, do you know what? It was bound to be Mrs Sciurus!'

Mrs Sciurus looked horrifyingly at the songbirds standing in front of her and then up at Judge Strix, still clutching her three babies for dear life. She felt faint. 'I swear I didn't do any of those things. I promise!'

'Silence! You'll get your turn to speak!' Judge Strix cried. 'If I'm feeling generous that is,' he said under his breath, with a smirk. 'Now, please, Head Athene,' he cried, lifting a wing in the direction of the little owls. One of the little owls shifted and sat up.

'Thank you, your honour. Now...' he coughed, 'what evidence do you three witnesses have that Mrs Sciurus did indeed do these dreadful deeds? Mrs Rubecula please, if you may, please tell us how Mrs Sciurus was responsible for the loss of your eggs?'

'Well I popped away from ... my nest for a minute ... and my eggs ... all five of my beautiful cream-coloured eggs were there. But when I came back they were all broken. Every one of them. There were teeth marks on the shells, squirrel teeth marks. And then I saw the silhouette of a squirrel moving away in the tree canopy above, so it must've been her!'

'Did you, Mrs Rubecula, see it was definitely Mrs Sciurus?' the Head Athene asked.

'Well, no, but it was a squirrel. I'm sure it was her alright!'

'It wasn't me ... I swear!' Mrs Sciurus cried out.

'Quiet!' Judge Strix boomed. 'Otherwise you will be removed without a fair trial!'

'This is a fair trial?' Mrs Sciurus gasped.

'It's the only trial you're getting! Now please, Head Athene, you may continue.'

Next, the head little owl asked Mr Sitta, followed by Major Parus, about how they were sure that it was Mrs Sciurus who had stripped the bark clean off the tree and broken the bird feeder to eat all the food. Both songbirds were united in their responses. 'Squirrel teeth marks, your honour. Unmistakable. It must've been her alright!'

Mrs Sciurus was about to say something else, but Judge Strix raised a wing and thanked the Head Athene for his questions. It was now time for the jury to make their decision. 'Shall you need much time?' the judge asked, looking across at the hoard of animals, which consisted of Mrs Vulgaris (the red squirrel), Mr Lutra (the otter), Miss Erina (the hedgehog) and Mr Arvicola (the water vole).

Mrs Sciurus watched as the four animals got in a huddle and, after only two seconds, Mrs Vulgaris stood in front, looked at Judge Strix and called up, 'We have a unanimous decision, your honour.'

'OK, on the charge of overstaying your welcome and not being wanted here, I have already concluded that you, Mrs Sciurus, and your family are guilty. In addition, Mrs Vulgaris, what is the jury's decision on the charge of Mrs Sciurus monstrously devouring poor Mrs Rubecula's eggs, debarking Mr Sitta's tree and destroying Major Parus's feeder?'

With a sly smile, the red squirrel looked at Mrs Sciurus and answered, 'On all three counts, your honour, the jury finds Mrs Sciurus guilty!'

Chapter 7
Help From Above

'I promise I didn't,' Mrs Sciurus cried out

'What does that mean, Mum?' Nip asked nervously, staring up at his mum.

'What it means...' Judge Strix boomed down, now standing fully upright, 'is that you far down there, yes that's right, you four grey vermin, are leaving this countryside instantly. And see that as me being lenient, as you could have had a much greater punishment. You barbarically ate Mrs Rubecula's eggs, severely vandalised Mr Sitta's tree and did irreversible damage to a feeder, which acted as an important food resource to many members of the local bird community!'

'No!' Mrs Sciurus cried out, putting her head in her paws.

'No, she didn't!' came a high pitched voice from above.

'Excuse me?' the judge asked. He looked up, puzzled. The whole room looked up. 'Who speaks and defies me in my court?!'

'Me, up here, and Mrs Sciurus didn't do any of those things, because I saw who done it!'

Just then a bat appeared from a cavity on the ceiling.

'Oh, ignore that stupid thing!' Judge Strix yelled. 'He doesn't know what he's talking about!'

'Yes, exactly, that's the problem with you lot. You

blame animals like Mrs Sciurus and me for things and make us the enemy just because we're different!'

'Don't be so stupid!' Judge Strix snapped. 'We don't like you because ... well ... you're not a bird or a proper mammal ... you're a mammal but with wings ... you're just weird! You're not normal! As for Mrs Sciurus, well, we don't like her because she committed a number of heinous crimes and the jury has decided she did them!'

'That jury?!' the bat laughed, looking down at the four animals. 'No wonder they decided that. For a start, one of them was the real culprit! Your actual monster is Mrs Vulgaris, I saw her do it. She puts the vulgar in VULGARis!'

Chapter 8
Battle Lines Are Drawn

The red squirrel gulped and was suddenly turning a little redder than usual. She was about to reply when Judge Strix lifted a wing.

'Please...' he nodded at her. 'Don't honour that with a response, Mrs Vulgaris. I've had enough. Major and Minor Dendrocopos, get him!'

Both black and white woodpeckers flew up and headed for the bat.

'Right, lads! Attack!' the bat called.

Suddenly, hundreds of bats started to fly down from the ceiling. They intercepted the woodpeckers and started to swarm around Judge Strix, the Athenes, Lieutenant Lepus and the other hares. Confusion and chaos erupted. It was quite a scene!

Meanwhile, the first bat landed beside Mrs Sciurus. 'You must run, now! Follow me!' The bat turned around and flew for the exit which was now unattended.

Mrs Sciurus gained her composure and looked down at her babies. 'Right, little ones. We need to go! Quick! Come on, come on!' With that, the grey squirrel family followed the bat across the room and out of the exit.

'Quick, they're getting away!' cried Judge Strix.

The head hare turned around and saw the back of the Sciurus family leaving. He smiled. The chase was on; and if anyone liked a chase, it was Lieutenant Lepus.

Chapter 9
Off Like a Bat Out of Hell!

Mrs Sciurus and her little ones followed the leading bat up an incline and reached the hole from the tree to the outside world. The bat stopped in mid-air.

'This is where I leave you, Mrs Sciurus.'

'How can I thank you?' she asked.

'No need m'lady. I couldn't let you take the blame for something you didn't do. Besides, you've as much right to live here as they have and don't let anyone tell you different.'

'Well, thank you very much, my little friend,' Mrs Sciurus said, softly touching the bat's small face with her paw. 'I never even got your name,' she said.

'Pipistrellus ma'am, but call me Pip for short, as we probably don't have time for you to call me Pipistrellus with these hares coming fast!'

'Hey, you can't be called Pip as well,' cried Pip. 'I'm Pip!' the little squirrel yelped.

'Fancy that!' Pipistrellus said. 'Well, this world is big enough for two Pips I think,' he laughed.

Just then there was a noise from behind them and they all turned around. Lieutenant Lepus and the group of hares were almost on them.

'Quickly, quickly!' Pipistrellus shouted. 'You go down

the old holly hedge. I'll distract this lot!' With that, the
bat shot back down into the tree.

Mrs Sciurus looked around. Her heart was racing.
'Come on little ones!' She put her arm around Pip, Kip
and Nip and picked them up. Then the Sciurus family
jumped out of the tree and scurried down towards the
old holly hedge.

Chapter 10
Heading For the Holly

Mrs Sciurus looked over her shoulder. The hare crew was gaining, with Lieutenant Lepus still leading the charge. The hares were super quick, much quicker than squirrels like Mrs Sciurus and the fact that she was half carrying, half dragging the rest of her family was slowing her down even more.

The hares were now only 100 metres away, then 80 metres, then 50 metres, then 30 metres, then 10 metres. They were gaining fast! The holly swung to the right and, as Mrs Sciurus scurried around the corner, she heard something on the other side of the hedge.

'Psst.'

She thought she must've been imagining it, but then,

all of a sudden, she heard it again.

'Psst ... don't go so fast,' came a voice. 'Over here. Come in here.'

Mrs Sciurus looked in front of her and to the right and suddenly saw the large pied head of a badger peering out from the bottom of the hedge.

'Quickly, through you come, before they see you,' it said.

Mrs Sciurus looked back. The hares were still around the corner, but she could hear their rapid footsteps fast approaching. It was her only option. She held onto Pip, Kip and Nip tightly and dived for the hole where the badger was. She got through to the other side just before she heard the hares stomp past, none the wiser, and head away down the holly hedge. Gradually, the footsteps got quieter and quieter. She puffed out, looked down, cuddled her little ones and gave a sigh of relief. When she looked up, there in front of them stood a badger and a red fox.

'Well, good day, Mrs Sciurus,' the badger said. 'Let me introduce ourselves. I'm Meles and my acquaintance here is Vulpes and we're both most delighted to meet you!'

Chapter 11
Meles and Vulpes

Mrs Sciurus was slightly hesitant. She had always been told to avoid badgers and foxes and that nothing good ever came of either of them. She clutched her little ones tightly and they gripped onto their mum even tighter.

'Please, Mrs Sciurus, you shouldn't be afraid,' Vulpes said, sensing her nerves. 'Why, the very reason that you're scared of us is precisely the reason why the other animals have a dislike for you my dear. Prejudice and stereotype.'

'Pure and simple!' Meles added.

'You see...' he continued. 'We're like you, Mrs Sciurus; we're a bit like outsiders too. A lot of animals distrust us; me, because I come out after dark, and my dear fellow Vulpes because he always gets blamed when young go missing; you know, chicks, eggs, that kind of thing. They think he eats anything that moves, but see, he hasn't eaten me yet!'

'And, anyway, Meles, my old friend, I'm just as satisfied eating an apple or two, or indeed dining at the Black Bin-bag Café on the scraps therein!' Vulpes declared.

Mrs Sciurus just stood there, watching these two animals. She loosened her grip on her little ones as she found herself trusting Vulpes and Meles more and more with every passing second.

Meles then piped up, 'There are a number of elements to gaining acceptance, my dear, and we've got a few ideas as to how we can help you!'

Chapter 12
Seeing Red!

'Firstly, the main thing, my dear, is to be yourself, to be a helpful member of society, but, as you know, it is sometimes not as simple as just that. Some animals around here will feel like you're treading on their paws. Jealously can be a terrible thing,' Meles said.

'But of course,' an animated Vulpes announced taking over, 'some other animals are full to the brim with prejudice, are rotten to the core with prejudice, and they only judge based on appearance and where you come from regardless of who you are!'

'So,' an even more animated badger interjected, 'to overcome this initial hurdle, we must think outside the box slightly and consider how we can get some of the other animals to embrace you in the first instance. A foot in the door if you like, so they can all get to see you for what you really are, without dismissing you instantly for just how you look and where you're from.' At this point the badger and the fox went quiet, each resting his head on a paw.

After a few seconds, the fox spoke. 'I have just the idea, my good friend Meles,' he announced, jumping forwards. 'For part of this, there's just one simple concoction: Row-Haw-Rose-Mud-Row-Row-Haw-Rose-Mud-Row!' he sang, to the tune of 'Row, row, row your boat'.

'Pardon?!' Meles and Mrs Sciurus asked together.

'Bear with me!'

'I beg your pardon, Vulpes? I'm a badger not a bear!' Meles cried.

'I mean be patient with me!'

With that, Vulpes skipped across to the hedge and took a handful of red berries from one bush, before dancing across to another and picking some more red berries, singing as he went about his work. He was brilliantly bonkers! After several minutes he returned in front of Mrs Sciurus.

'Hands please,' he requested. 'Out in front like they're cupped for holding water.'

'What, like this?'

'Yes, perfect,' Vulpes sang, dropping the collection of berries into her hands. 'And finally, Meles, some of that lovely mud please!'

'What, this stuff?' he asked, digging his shovel-like paws into the ground and lifting a pile of damp gloopy mud into the air.

'Just the stuff, please, if you don't mind.' He actioned towards Mrs Sciurus's cupped hands and Meles plonked the mud into her paws.

'I do mind! Excuse me!' she cried.

'No, excuse me,' Vulpes laughed 'Row-Haw-Rose-Mud-Row-Row-Haw-Rose-Mud-Row. A handful of ROWan berries, a fistful of HAWthorn berries, a pinch of ROSE hips and a good splattering of mud; a few extra ROWans and repeat. It may just help a bit with your slight problem!' He snapped a stick off a nearby bush and started to mash and stir the reddy-brown gloop in Mrs Sciurus's paws.

'You're making a mess of my hands. You're turning them red!' Mrs Sciurus shouted.

'Why, that is the intention, dear,' Vulpes exclaimed. 'Red is the new grey!'

Over the next few minutes the Sciurus family were all converted to distinctively red-looking squirrels.

'Almost there. Oh, one more thing,' Vulpes cried, rushing forward and fluffing up Mrs Sciurus's ears, and then the little ones' ears, one by one. 'I almost forgot the ear tufts!'

Meles and Vulpes stepped back and placed an arm around each other. Meles spoke first, with a chortle. 'My dear Vulpes, they say I put the bad in BADger, but you certainly put the sly in SLY fox, my old chum.'

Chapter 13
Fairing Up For the Fair

'Next, Mrs Sciurus, at least initially, if you want to be like a red squirrel, you must eat like a red squirrel,' Vulpes announced. 'This, my dear, is a pine cone,' he said, breaking the cone in his paws. 'And this is a pine nut. Enjoy!' he said with a smile, and he threw the nut to Mrs Sciurus. She nibbled on it. It tasted nothing like the delicious acorns she was most used to and there was considerably less eating in them too. Her tummy groaned with hunger.

'Finally, my dear, we shall work on your agility and on spending less time on the ground and more time up there,' he said, pointing up a tree. 'Red squirrels are

always up there, a bit more so than you, no doubt. Up you get. I want to see you jump between that tree and that one and that one and that one...' Vulpes was spinning around pointing at tree after tree as he bobbed up and down.

Mrs Sciurus sighed, but, as she felt she could trust these two marvellous mammals, this became her daily routine for the next week and the squirrel family stayed with Vulpes over this time. Before long Mrs Sciurus was looking decidedly more like a red squirrel.

Then, one fine morning, one week later, Meles visited Vulpes at his home, the earth.

After initial pleasantries between the badger, fox and Mrs Sciurus, Meles turned to Vulpes and said, 'My dear friend, with the village fair on today I think it would be an excellent time to introduce Mrs Sciurus and her family back to the local community.'

'Why, I think that is a wonderful idea, my dear Meles, but remember that we will not be welcome to the fair by the other animals.'

'Oh, can't you come too?' Mrs Sciurus asked, her little ones looking up at Meles and Vulpes expectantly.

'No, Vulpes is right my dear, but, fear not, for we are old and thick-skinned and will not let other animals' misplaced dislike and distrust affect us.'

'You can be sure of that,' Vulpes added, looking at Mrs Sciurus with a wink.

'Right, let's go!' Meles cried out. 'You, Mrs Sciurus, have a fair to attend!'

Chapter 14
Meles and Vulpes Bow Out

Meles led the way, followed by Vulpes and then Mrs Sciurus with her little ones.

They moved through a woodland thicket and under a canopy of ash, sycamore and oak trees, before passing through one wheat field, then another and then another. After a little while, Mrs Sciurus heard many voices in front of them. They were coming from the other side of a thick blackthorn hedge.

'Here we are,' Meles announced, stopping by the hedge.

'We leave you now, my dear,' Vulpes sighed.

'Really?' Mrs Sciurus asked.

'Yes, it's time for you to start your new chapter. To get back on with your life, here where you belong. Remember, Mrs Sciurus. The main thing is that you be you. Acceptance isn't about how you look. It's about what you do and how you behave, even if some of the animals around here don't think so. That's why you're looking a bit more red than usual. You need an initial help to get over the first prejudice hurdle, but, remember, it's what you do afterwards that really matters, my dear.'

'I don't know how to thank you.'

'No need to thank us,' Meles said. 'It's just not right that they don't accept you because you're different. They need to appreciate you for being you. And some already do, like us.'

'The village fair awaits you, dear Mrs Sciurus. Enjoy yourself and we'll see you around,' Vulpes said. He bowed in front of the squirrels, followed by Meles.

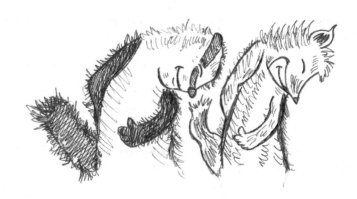

Mrs Sciurus looked in the direction of the joyous voices over the hedge and turned back to Vulpes and Meles. There was now only empty spaces where they had been standing. They were gone. It was only then that Mrs Sciurus realised how much she had enjoyed their company. She felt a tinge of sadness that she and her babies were all alone again. If only Mr Sciurus was here with them. If only he was here to give her that reassuring squeeze of her paw with his that he used to. She took a deep breath, put her arms around Pip, Kip and Nip, and walked through a gap in the hedge and down to the fair.

Chapter 15
Fun at the Fair

As the Sciurus family walked through the crowd of animals - hares, water voles, otters and hedgehogs, to name a few - Mrs Sciurus was amazed at the number who spoke.

'Hello m'lady,' said a hedgehog politely bowing his head.

'Beautiful morning ma'am,' said a hare.

'Hello, gorgeous!' shouted an over-friendly otter.

'My, my,' Mrs Sciurus said, smiling and looking down at Pip, Kip and Nip, who all had smiles from ear tuft to ear tuft. When she looked back up she noticed an ageing mole struggling with a large box. 'Oh, please, allow me,' Mrs Sciurus said taking the box from the mole.

'Oh, why, thank you, my dear.'

'Now, where are we going?'

'Oh my home is five minutes over this way. Up and over the hill, if you don't mind, dear?'

'Of course not. Can I ask what's in here?'

'Let's just say I got lucky with the raffle,' the mole chuckled.

After helping the old mole and returning to the fair, the little ones had a shot on the merry-go-round, then the dodgems and then the coconut shy.

Meanwhile, Mrs Sciurus was madly rushing around helping other older animals with the prizes they had won. She had a new lease of life. Who knew being a red squirrel could be such fun!

'You're such a lovely dear,' all the animals would say to her, after she had helped them.

Next, she was asked to lend a paw running a stall. 'I just need to pop down to the river and catch some lunch. Are you OK holding the fort?' the otter asked.

'Oh, yes, of course.'

'Won't be long.'

'Take as long as you want,' Mrs Sciurus chirped.

Then, finally, when the goalkeeper, a red squirrel, was injured when playing 'Beat the Squirrely Goalie', he turned to Mrs Sciurus. 'You don't mind taking my place, do you?'

'Why, of course not,' she replied with glee. She h
never been a goalkeeper before but how hard could
be? Just try and save the acorn.

Mrs Sciurus was having the best day of her life. Th
fair was just marvellous. Unlike the weather, however
which was changing fast, for the worse!

Chapter 16. A Wash Out!

. you for helping out,' the red squirrel said to Mrs
us, after she had saved the last acorn of the day.

nytime, my friend,' Mrs Sciurus replied, skipping
k to the coconut shy where Pip, Kip and Nip were
aying.

'Right, kids. I think it's time we best be off.'

'Awwww, Mum. We're having so much fun though!'
Pip, Kip and Nip cried out.

'But we have our dinner to get, little ones.'

Reluctantly, the little ones followed their mum out of
the fair.

'Oh, excuse me, dear, would you mind helping me
with this?' said an elderly hare, who was standing there
with a glass container which held the largest carrot
cake Mrs Sciurus had ever seen.

'Yes, of course, but only if I can have a slice of it,' she
laughed. 'Which way are we going?' she asked, taking
the container from the grateful hare.

'Oh, back up to the fair, my dear, if that's not too
much trouble?'

'Of course not.' With that, Mrs Sciurus, Pip, Kip and
Nip walked with the old hare, Mrs Sciurus holding his
frail arm for support.

Just then the heavens opened and rain started to
pour down. It was coming down hard. Mrs Sciurus

looked up. It just looked like one large thunder cl.
The squirrels and the hare hurriedly walked throu
the crowd, which was starting to disperse.

Mrs Sciurus tried to shelter the little ones unde
her arms. She was drenched. She looked down to see
whether Pip, Kip and Nip were managing to stay dry
and that's when she noticed. She gasped in horror!

Her little ones were no longer red, for the rain had
washed the colour off. She looked down at her own paw,
then arms, then body - she was no longer red either!

Chapter 17
,rue Colours Shining Through

,'re very kind to help me like this. I never got your ,me, dear?' the old hare asked, but Mrs Sciurus wasn't ,istening. They had to get away before anyone noticed. AND FAST!

Unfortunately, it was too late and there was a loud, 'Ehm, excuse me,' from behind them.

'Oh no,' she thought, as she turned around to see Lieutenant Lepus standing there with his arms folded.

'So, we do meet again!' he barked.

The old hare looked around at Lepus and then to Mrs Sciurus. 'What's the matter, son?' he asked.

'What's the matter, Dad, is that escorting you to the fair is not a red squirrel at all, it's a grey squirrel!'

'And?'

'What do you mean AND?!' Lepus boomed.

'This charming dear has been very nice to me and has offered to help me get here, which is more than can be said for you!' the old hare shot back.

Lepus had no answer to his father.

With the raised voices, quite a crowd was now surrounding Mrs Sciurus. She only just noticed that the rain had gone, the thunder cloud had passed and the sun was back out. It didn't feel very warming though.

She now felt cold and a chill made her shake.

'Well, we'll see what Judge Strix thinks of this!' Lepus barked.

'Someone wanted me?' The large owl swooped down from a tree high above.

'Yes, me, judge. Guess what?! Mrs Sciurus! She's back!'

'Oh, yes, indeed. So I see,' Judge Strix said, eyeing up Mrs Sciurus. As the little ones cuddled their mother, she shivered, one of her paws still holding the elderly hare's cake and her other the old creature's arm.

The owl moved back and forth in front of the squirrel family, with his head moving in a comical circular motion from side to side. He was thinking the situation through and there was hush from the crowd as Judge Strix stayed quiet.

The owl walked forward and stood in front of the sodden squirrel family. His face still wore a strict and stern expression, as it had throughout the time in his court a week before. Lepus stood beside Judge Strix with a huge smile on his face, readying himself for the sure-fire trouble which was about to begin.

Mrs Sciurus half closed her eyes fearing the worst, but, when she peered through, she thought she noticed a slight change in Judge Strix's expression.

Chapter 18
Caring For the Community

'Why, what have we here?' Judge Strix said turning to the old hare.

'She's been a fabulous dear and helped me get to the fair with my cake. She's been terrific, judge. An absolute star.'

'Really?'

'And she helped me carry my prizes home,' called a hedgehog, stepping proudly forward to be beside Mrs Sciurus.

'And helped me with my stall,' an otter cried out, smiling at Mrs Sciurus.

'And helped me with "Beat the Goalie",' said a red squirrel, putting his arm around Mrs Sciurus. She smiled as she looked around at the beaming faces of the other animals. Judge Strix looked into the crowd thoughtfully.

Lepus shuffled uncomfortably, 'But, judge!' he cried out. 'She's not like you and me! She's not from around here! Not really! She's different! She's not wanted here!'

Judge Strix paused for a moment and collected his thoughts. What was said next, Mrs Sciurus could hardly believe. 'And does that matter, Lieutenant Lepus? Does it really matter where Mrs Sciurus is from? In fact, does it matter where any one of us is from? Besides, I think you might be mistaken that she's not wanted,' he exclaimed as he surveyed the happy crowd.

'What the...? Listen, judge, she needs to go!' Lepus spat. His eyes were mad with anger as he stepped in front of Judge Strix and stared right into his face.

'Step away!' Judge Strix boomed back 'Why, Mrs Sciurus has done more for this community this afternoon than you have done in a lifetime. If you don't like it, then you know what you can do!' he called, raising a wing and pointing away.

'I can't believe this!' the hare fumed. Lepus leered at Judge Strix again, but he maintained the same stern stare.

'Right, I've had enough of this place!' Lepus called out, stepping away from the judge. 'Come on, who's with me?' He looked at the crowd. No-one moved. He paused and started to fidget frantically. 'Dad, come on, I'll help you with your stuff!'

'No, you don't worry yourself. Why start now? I'm doing very well here, thank you,' the old hare replied, still holding Mrs Sciurus's arm.

'Well ... you can all go to hell!' Lepus boomed and he marched through the crowd, glaring at Mrs Sciurus as he stormed past.

'Good riddance to that. From now on, this community will do very well, I suspect, without that attitude, downright prejudice and negativity!' Judge Strix declared. 'Right, Mrs Sciurus. I believe the cake contest is to start shortly. How would you and your little ones like to be judges?'

'Yeah!' Pip yelled.

Mrs Sciurus smiled and looked at Judge Strix. 'But I thought you were the judge?' she asked chuckling.

'Let me be the judge of that!' the owl laughed back.

'No, seriously, we'd love to,' Mrs Sciurus added.

'I believe walnut cake is the most common this year.'

'Oh, wonderful,' replied Mrs Sciurus, cuddling the little ones 'Although I think we might've already found our favourite,' she smiled, looking down at the carrot cake and then to the old hare who was still supported by her arm. He smiled back.

'Ehm, actually ... I hope you don't mind me asking, but we have two good friends who I'm sure would love to come into the fair too, if that's OK? They've never been before,' Mrs Sciurus asked. Pip, Kip and Nip looked up at their mum and smiled. They all knew exactly who she meant.

'Why, of course, Mrs Sciurus, the more the merrier!'

Mrs Sciurus smiled. 'Let's get this cake up to the contest, my friend,' she said, looking at the old hare. 'I'll go and fetch my two best friends afterwards.'

And, with that, Mrs Sciurus helped the old hare, as she walked with her family, Judge Strix and the rest of the animals back into the fair.

THE END

Dr Colin Bonnington

Colin works as an ecological consultant based in Manchester. He writes wildlife themed stories based on his experiences during his work. He completed a doctorate at the University of Sheffield on the impact of grey squirrels on birds, and still regularly writes scientific journal articles. 'The Grey Tale of Mrs Sciurus' is his first step into writing for children. Colin lives in Cheshire with his cat and his wife (and, at the moment, her baby bump!)

CPSIA information can be obtained
at www.ICGtesting.com
Printed in the USA
LVHW04s1324300418
575384LV00004B/589/P